GW00585978

CAPITAL T
WORTH GIVING A
CRAP ABOUT

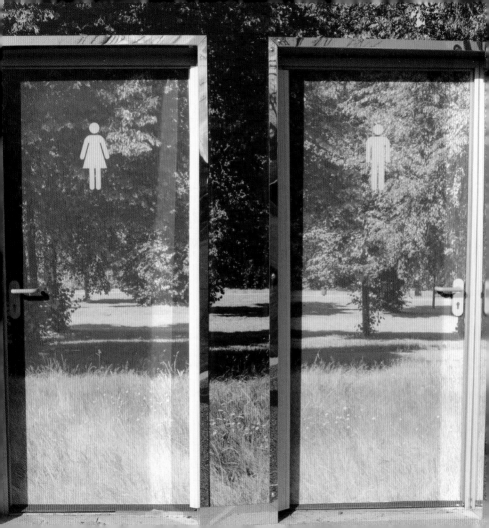

LOOS
OF
LONDON

LOOS OF LONDON

Ah, London! City of culture, global financial centre, historical Mecca and, yes, home to some of the weirdest, wackiest and most wonderful loos on the planet. You could say our great capital is number one in the world of number ones and twos. Where else could you pee while taking in a 40-mile view, poo where Queen Victoria, Edward VII and Churchill pooed, or have your offloadings serenaded by the speeches of Maggie Thatcher? And if piddling in unlikely places is your thing, why not let it go in an egg, a battleship, a prison, or underneath a Wesleyian chapel?

Then there are the loo conversions that have been so squeakily cleaned you can literally eat your dinner off them: subterranean former conveniences that now serve cocktails and charcuterie in thankfully well-scrubbed cubicles, a former courthouse that has turned shitty cells into a place fit for City swells, and even a public lav transformed into a posh private pad.

Londoners have been sharing their spoils since the Romans founded the city, bringing with them their toga-lifting toilet technology. Splashed among the 50 or so kicking khazis between this book's covers you will find fascinating facts and figures about two thousand years of cacking in the capital.

So next time you're caught short, give yourself and your toilet tackle a treat and try one of London's very best bogs. Or, if you're feeling flushed, why not test out the lot?

 Colour in or tick off this symbol as you travel around London finding the best bogs in town

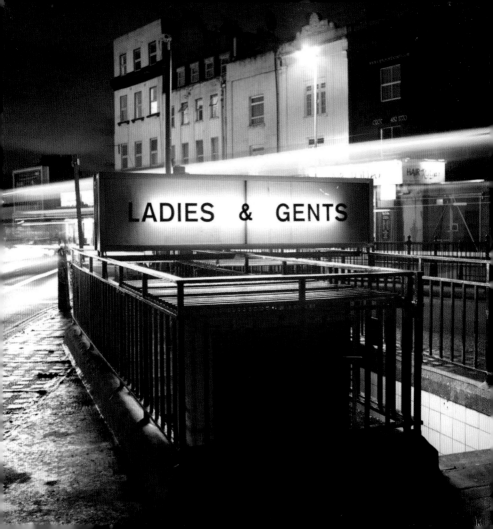

LADIES & GENTLEMEN

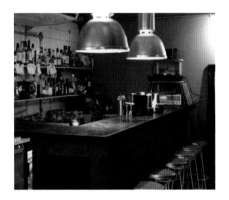

What's this? Some kind of space-saving unisex pissoir? Hold onto your tackle, it's actually a converted Victorian convenience in Kentish Town, where you can get lashed inside a loo, spending considerably more than a penny on a bar-full of craft vodkas and gins.

ladiesandgents.co

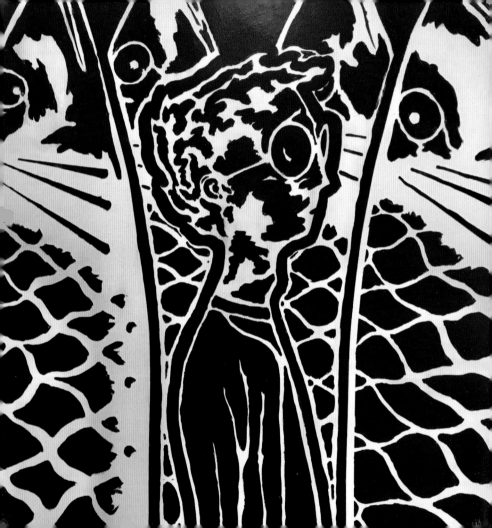

LONDON SHELL CO.

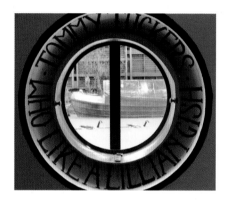

It's not every day that you can poo as you pass London Zoo, but you can do just that after stuffing yourself with Lillian Gish – fish – on the London Shell Co.'s Regent's Canal barge. So, fetch out your own little Tommy Tucker and take a Jimmy Riddle as you watch the world, and a selection of shopping trolleys, float by.

londonshellco.com

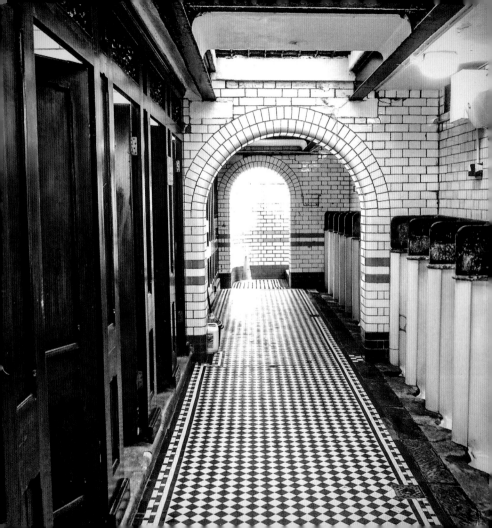

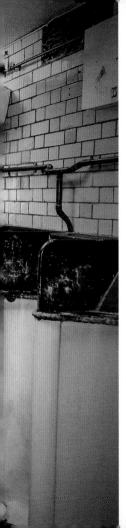

SOUTH END GREEN

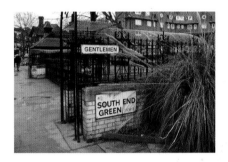

How do you squeeze 16 men into a loo?
Take them to South End Green and
give them a urinal each, to pee freely
in Victorian lavvy splendour. The public
convenience, a bog-roll's throw from
Hampstead Heath, was built in 1897 for
the relief of caught-short tram passengers,
and plenty was splashed out on porcelain,
marble and tiling. It's a celebrity crapper,
too, cruised by the playwright Joe Orton
in the 1960s and the scene of a few of
George Michael's 'careless whispers'.

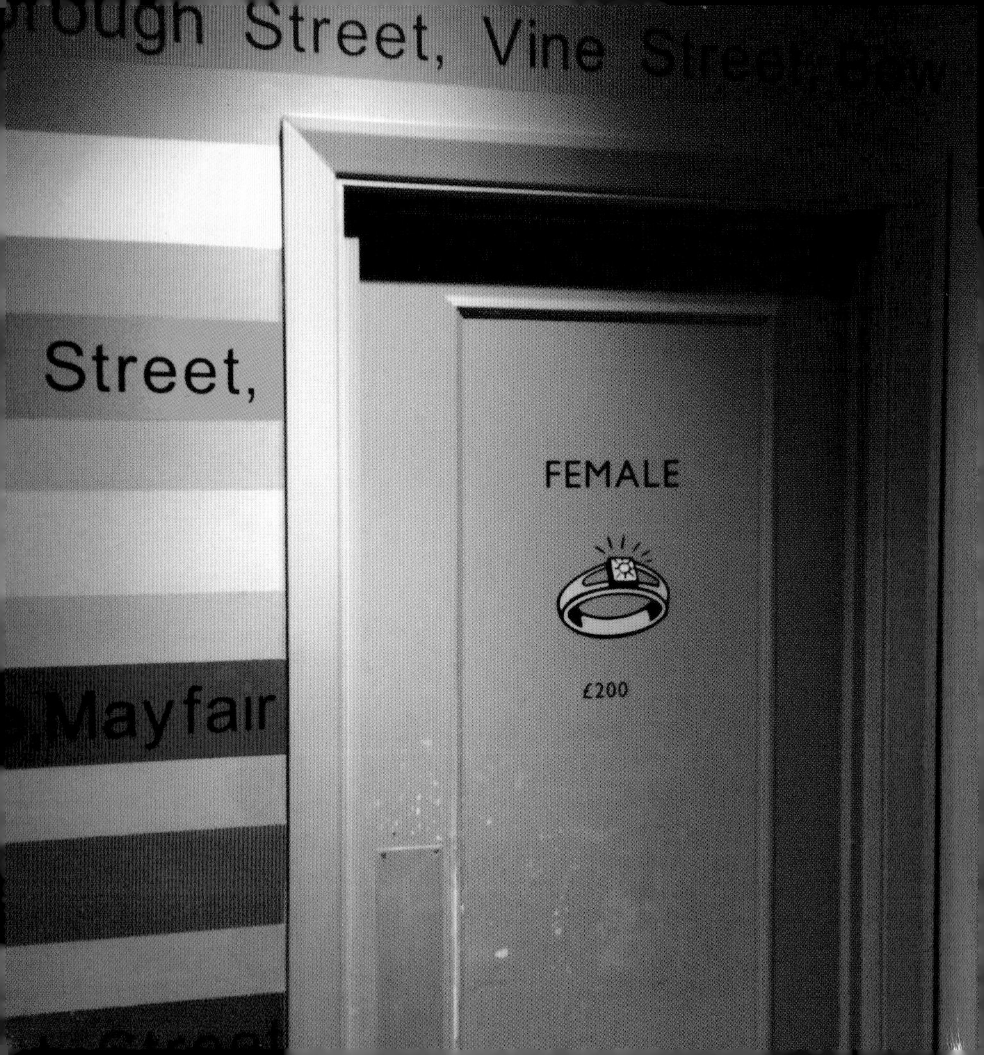

rough Street, Vine Street,
Street,
Mayfair
FEMALE
£200

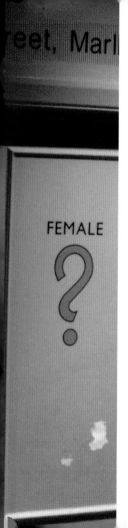

FEMALE

THE CASTLE

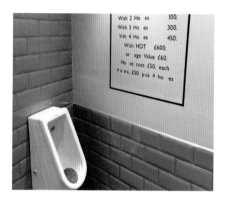

With 2 Ho es   100.
With 3 Ho es   300.
With 4 Ho es   450.
With HOT   £600.
or age Value £60.
Ho es cost £50. each
Ho es, £50. p us 4 ho es

If you get caught short on the Pentonville
Road (yours for £120), pop into The Castle
pub and have your waterworks sorted the
Monopoly way. 'Females' can put a ring on
it or take a chance, and there's free parking
for all. Careful who you show your utilities to,
though, or you might end up in jail.

thecastleislington.co.uk

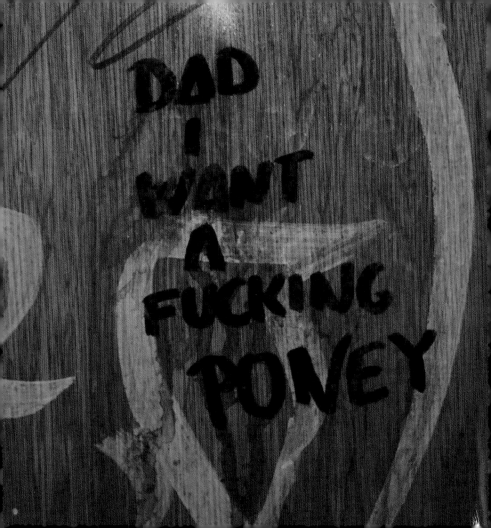

THE THRONE ROOM

The Queen is never far from a royal wee. More than 10 per cent of the rooms in Buckingham Palace are bathrooms: 78 out of 775.

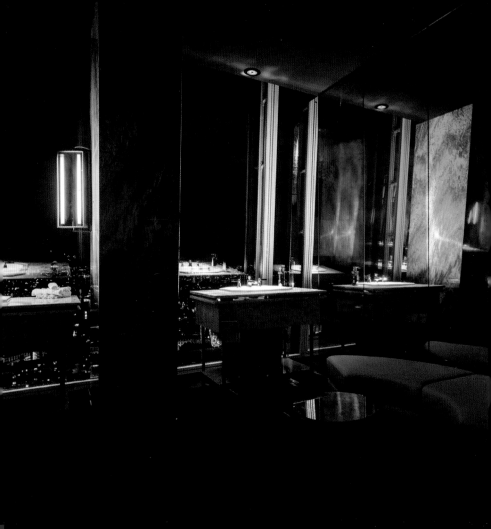

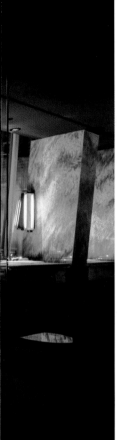

AQUA SHARD

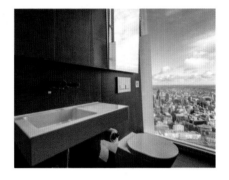

See the lights twinkle as you take a tinkle.
In the gents at the Aqua Shard restaurant
you can piss on London from a great height
– the 31st floor of the Shard, to be precise,
the UK's largest erection at 309.7m (1,016ft).

aquashard.co.uk

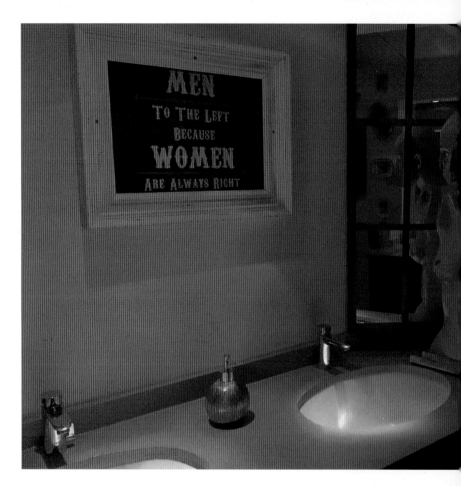

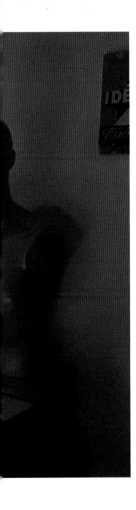

BORO BISTRO

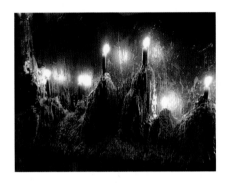

Ooh là là! If you like a surreal slash or a
Dalí-like dump, the freaky-chic loos at Boro
Bistro in Borough Market should tickle your
French fancy. That's if you can actually
find your way to the lav and locate the
necessaries in the low, louche light. If you
do, pull up a toilet seat, grab a candle and
while away your wazz admiring the weird
and wonderful décor.

borobistro.co.uk

JUBILOO

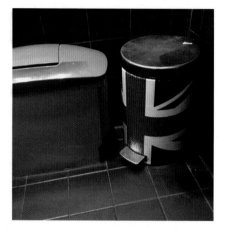

Where better to plant the great British bottom than on a seat in the Jubiloo public lav on the South Bank, with a great British bulldog watching your back – or front, when upstanding. The Union Jack is everywhere – loos, bins, mirrors – so run a flag up your pole and think of England.

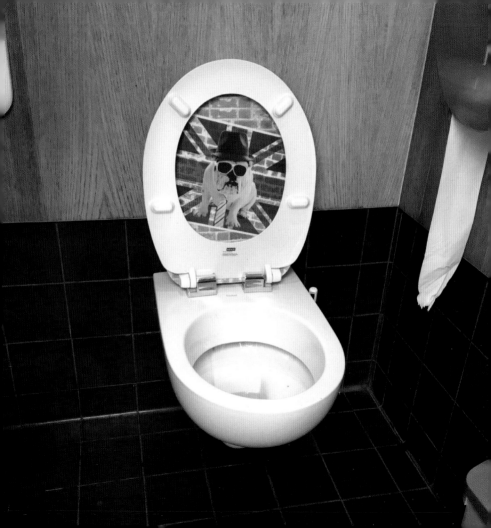

PRIVATE HOME, LAMBETH

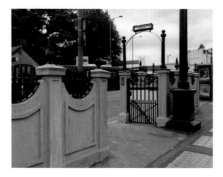

Who lives in a house like this? For a start,
someone who doesn't mind sharing space
with the ghosts of thousands of crappers
past, because, we shit you not, this smart,
architect-designed, one-bedroomed
Lambeth flat was once a public lav. Built
in 1929 and abandoned in the 1980s,
the derelict underground loo has been
transformed from dump to dream home.

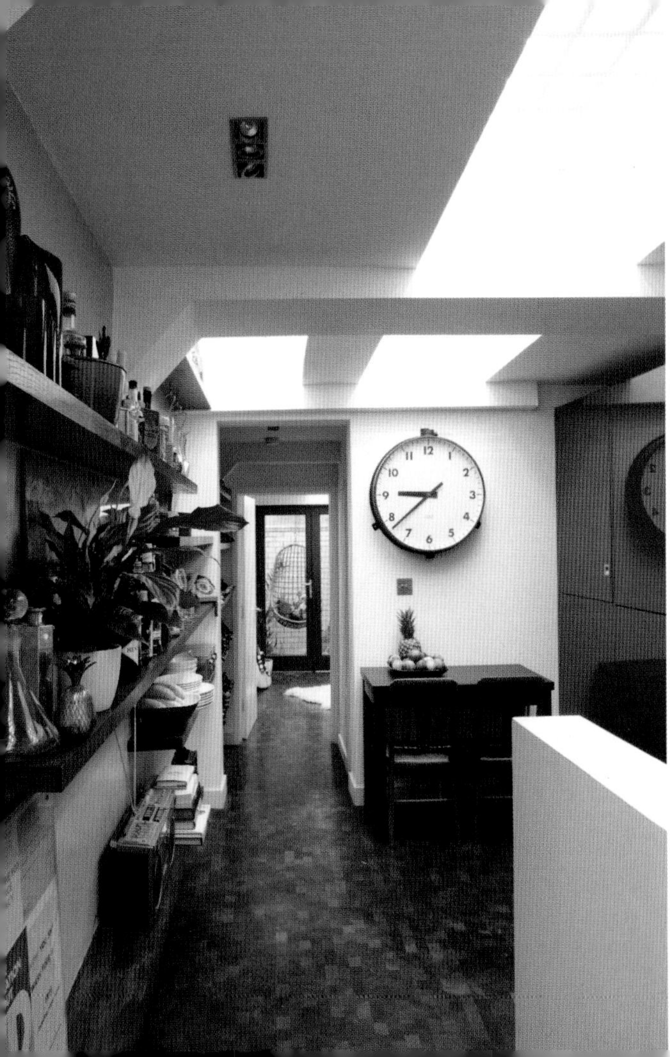

BANKERS FULL OF CRAP

A survey grandly named the
Great British Public Toilet Analysis,
launched in 2014, found that the
City of London, the UK's smallest
council area, had 108 public toilets:
the third-highest concentration in
the nation.

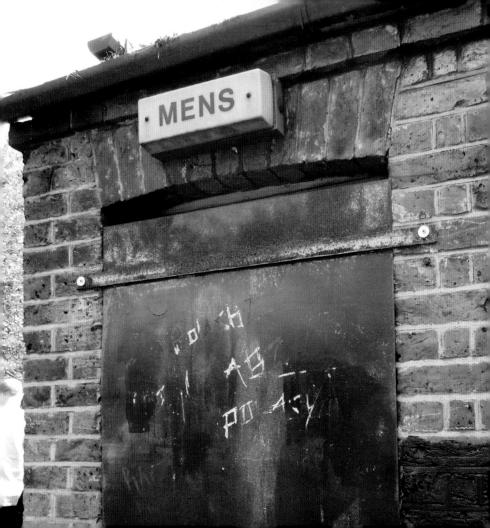

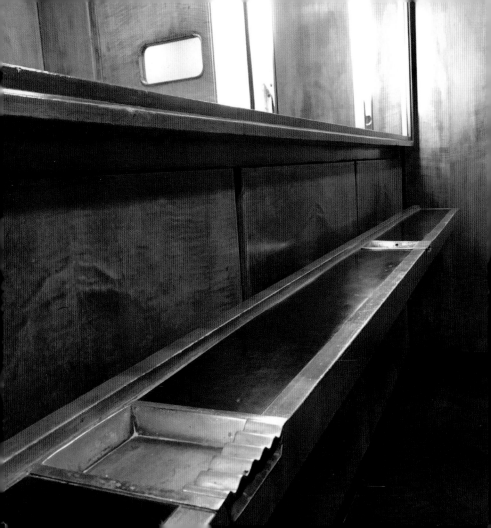

ROYAL FESTIVAL HALL

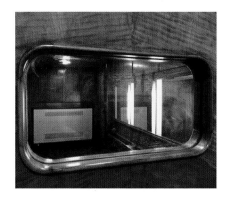

Ahoy there, shit-mates! If you like to poo like
you're on the *QE2*, then the nautical-looking
ladies at the Royal Festival Hall should
grab your gusset. By the way, that's a large
ashtray, gents, not the world's smallest urinal
with convenient ridges for hands-free peeing.

southbankcentre.co.uk

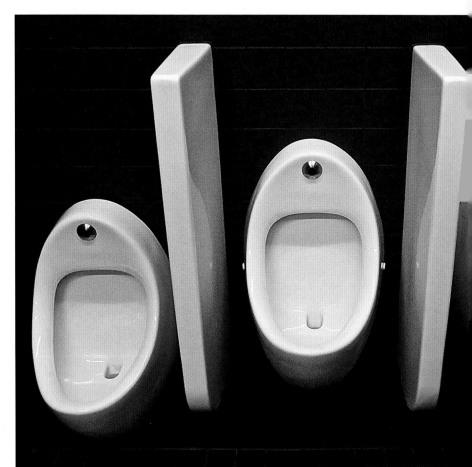

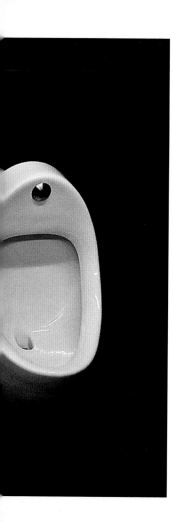

TATE MODERN

Create your own master-piss in
the arty-farty loos at the Tate
Modern. Stand in the middle
and your Gilbert and George will
be perfectly framed. Stand to the
left if you're a bit underfunded
in the Jackson Pollocks.
Stand wherever you like for a
guaranteed Ai Weiwei.

tate.org.uk

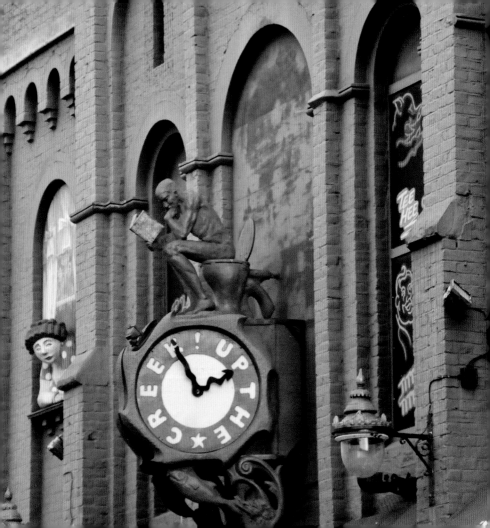

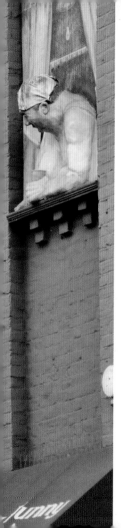

UP THE CREEK

Ever get the feeling, when you're propped
on the pooper, stark-bollock naked, reading
the *Beano*, that someone's watching you?
Well, the bronzed bloke atop Up the Creek
comedy club has the whole of Greenwich
passing by as he passes one out. Up Shit
Creek, and not a paddle in sight.

up-the-creek.com

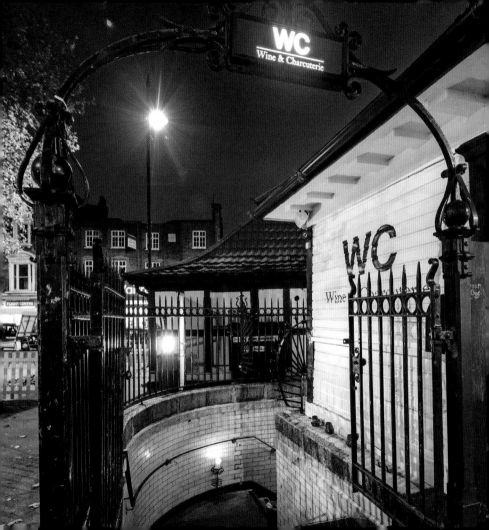

WC

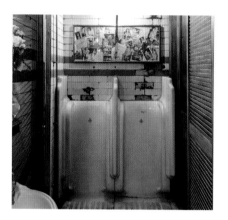

Ah, crapping by candelight! And what meat!
So, wrap your chops around a nice savoury
sausage and swig a Pee-no Grigio at WC
(Wine and Charcuterie – get it?), a food and
wine bar cunningly carved out of a century-
old public loo beneath Clapham Common
tube station.

wcclapham.co.uk

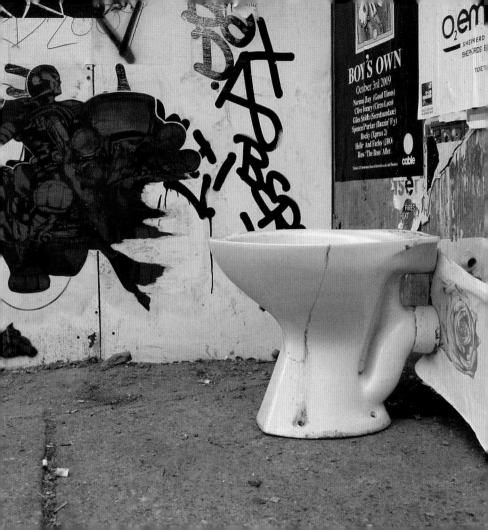

DON'T PISS YOUR LIFE AWAY!

The average loo-going Londoner makes 2,500 visits to the lav each year – that's three whole months over a lifetime – and uses almost 60 sheets of bog roll per day. That's a lot of paperwork.

THE ATTENDANT

There are stools, and then there are stools.
At The Attendant café in Victoria, converted
from an abandoned underground Victorian
convenience, you can sit on one and
contemplate the many thousands of Percys
that have been pointed at this Doulton &
Co. porcelain over more than a century.
Unsurprisingly, pulled pork is on the menu.

the-attendant.com

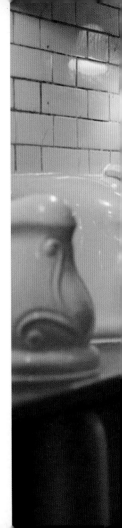

BUNGA BUNGA

It's the closest thing to taking a
pee in Pompeii. Enter the Bunga
Bunga restaurant loos in Covent
Garden to soak up an orgy of
marble, mosaics and mucky
murals, then hoist up the toga
and relieve yourself just like the
Romans did.

bungabunga-london.com

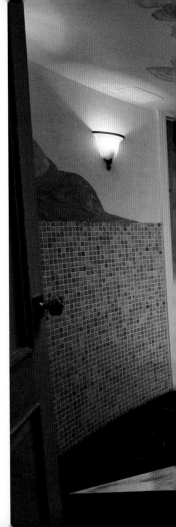

CABINET WAR ROOMS

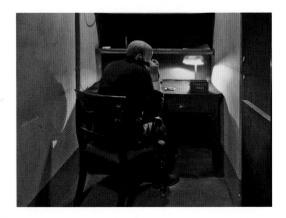

Hurry up, Winston, there's a queue! Yes, Churchill often locked himself in the bog-standard-looking toilet of the Cabinet War Rooms beneath Whitehall, but there were no leaks here. The cunningly disguised convenience actually housed a top-secret phone link that allowed Winnie to mentally unzip and pour his thoughts out to US President Roosevelt.

iwm.org.uk

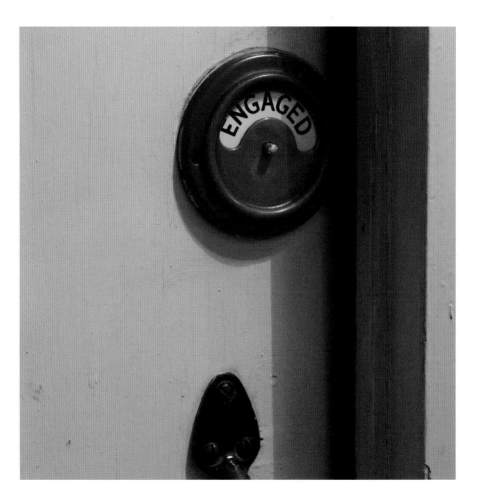

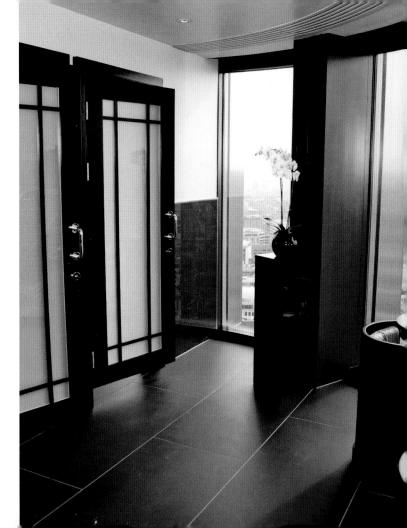

CITY SOCIAL

Why's she been so long in the bloody
toilet?! Well, at the City Social restaurant,
24 floors up Tower 42 in the City, it could
be the spectacular post-poo view over the
metropolis, or perhaps it's the dinky little
make-up tables, where she can adjust
lipstick, powder and paint to her heart's
delight until you've paid the bill.

citysociallondon.com

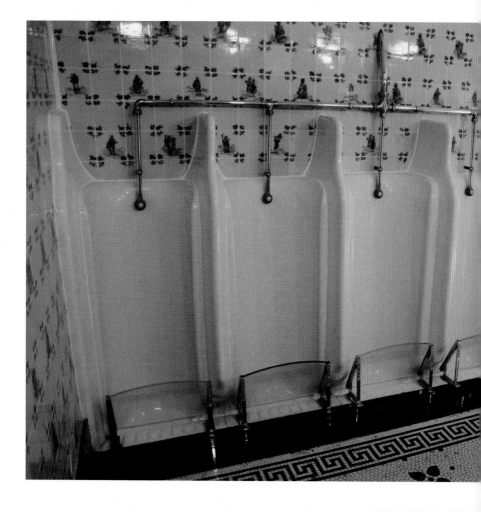

CLARIDGE'S

It's where all the big knobs
hang out. And the men's loo at
Claridge's hotel is just the place
for the poshest of pees against
porcelain perfection. All this,
and the guarantee of no piddle
on your pumps, thanks to the
cunningly placed splash-back
protectors. The guests here are
soaked only in money.

claridges.co.uk

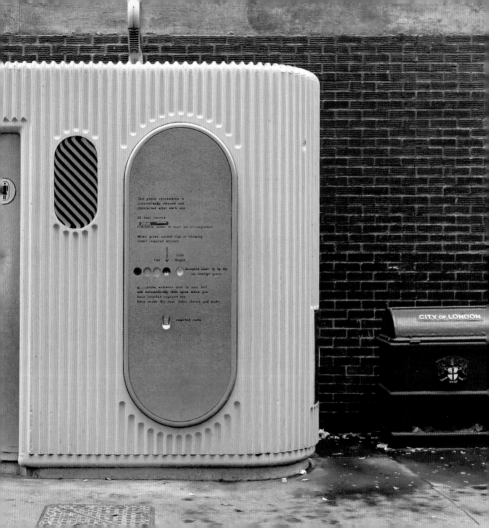

A TITANIC INCONVENIENCE

A mammoth 'fatberg' was discovered in the sewers below East London in September 2017. As heavy as 11 double-deckers and longer than Tower Bridge, the stinking mass was made up of cooking fats and food scraps, and flushed wet wipes, nappies and condoms. Nice.

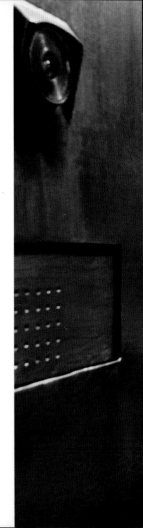

COURTHOUSE HOTEL

Perfect for ex-cons looking to recreate the
joys of dumping in front of fellow felons,
the bar at the West End's Courthouse
Hotel, once the Great Marlborough Street
Magistrates' Court, still has a khazi in the
corner of what was one of the holding cells.
If only that toilet bowl could speak … Mick
Jagger, Keith Richards and Johnny Rotten all
passed through on their way to drugs fines.

courthouse-hotel.com

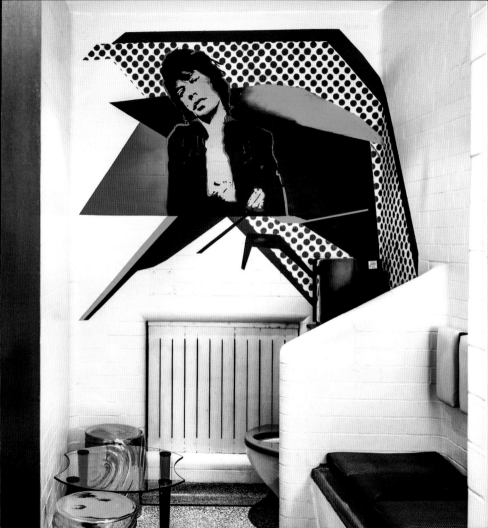

CUCKOO CLUB

Get face to face with a right
bunch of tits in the ladies' loo at
Mayfair's Cuckoo Club. They're
the work of 1970s style guru
Barbara Hulanicki, who founded
BIBA but has here gone all
Booby. It's pinker than a barrel
full of flamingos.

thecuckooclub.com

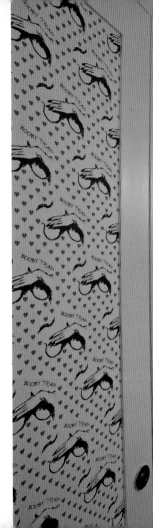

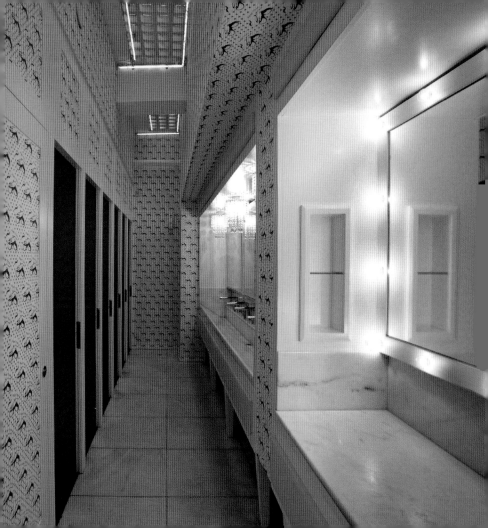

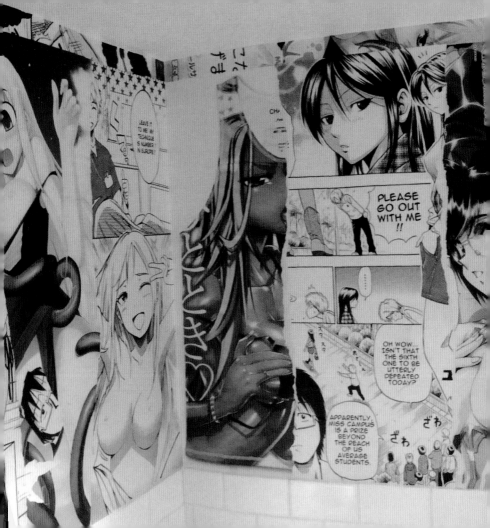

FLESH AND BUNS

Having sudoku'd yourself with steamed buns, sushi and sake in this Japanese-style gastropub in Covent Garden, make for the loos and feast your eyes on, well, a load of flesh and busty buns, manga-comic style. It's a ninja nipple-fest, guaranteed to test the concentration of any samurai swordsman.

bonedaddies.com

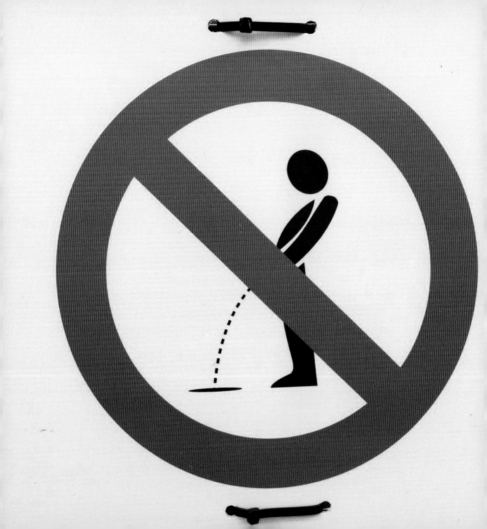

THE FIRST FLUSH OF SUCCESS

Tudor knight in tights Sir John Harington knew
a thing or two about waterworks.

The so-called 'saucy godson' of Elizabeth I
and ancestor of *Game of Thrones* actor
Kit invented the flushing toilet in 1596, and
even installed a throne room for his grateful
godmother at Richmond Palace. The 'privie
in perfection' required a whopping 60 pints of
water per flush, though Harington guaranteed
a good twenty sessions between flushes. 'And
this being well done, and orderly kept, your
worst privy may be as sweet as your best
chamber.' It did not catch on.

HAMLEYS

Wow! Need a toy-fuelled tinkle or a
playtime poo in Hamleys, the world's
oldest and largest fun store? Then pick a
radioactive colour and chocs away in the
ultimate kids' khazi. This is just the place
to act your shoe size, not your age. So
channel the inner Peter Pan, but keep the
aim low – and remember, it's not a toy.

hamleys.com

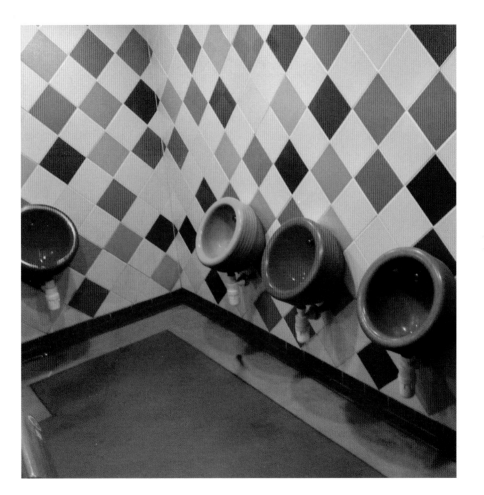

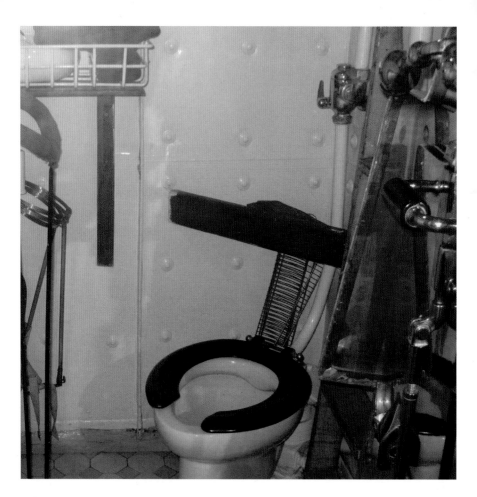

HMS *BELFAST*

No, it's not the enema room at some dodgy
S&M parlour. This is one of the plumbing-
heavy toilets on HMS *Belfast*, where you
can fire off a few broadsides in preparation
for your own Dump-Day landing. Use the
handy ladder to vary the trajectory and listen
out for calls to 'abandon shit!'

iwm.org.uk

THE HOSPITAL CLUB

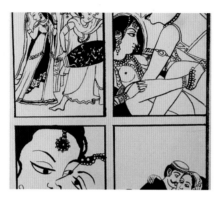

Taking a pee or poo at The Hospital Club
in Covent Garden can put you in a bit of
a position. One of many, as it happens,
depicted on the Kama Sutra'd cubicle
walls. But then, if you visit a private
club, you have to expect to meet some
prominent members. It's a lav to linger in
while you look and learn.

thehospitalclub.com

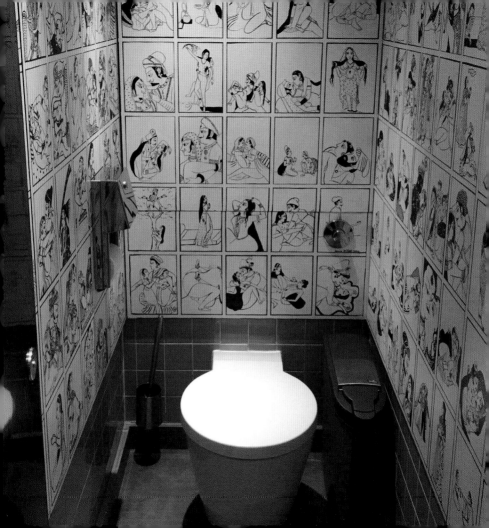

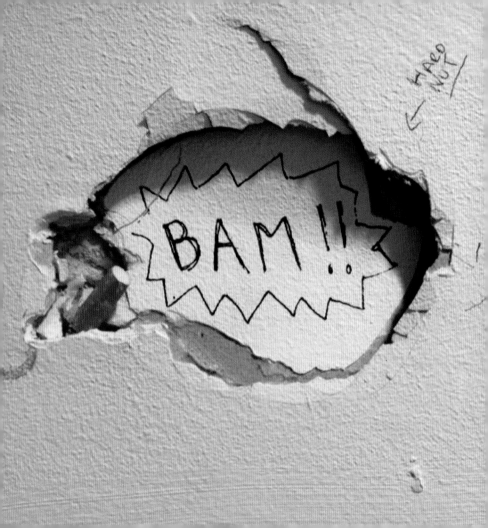

SOMETHING SMELLS FISHY ...

In the early days of household plumbing, when unfiltered water was piped in from London's rivers and ponds, it was not unusual to find unwelcome visitors swimming about in your precious supply. One resident of Pall Mall was horrified to discover a dozen eels almost two feet long in his waterworks.

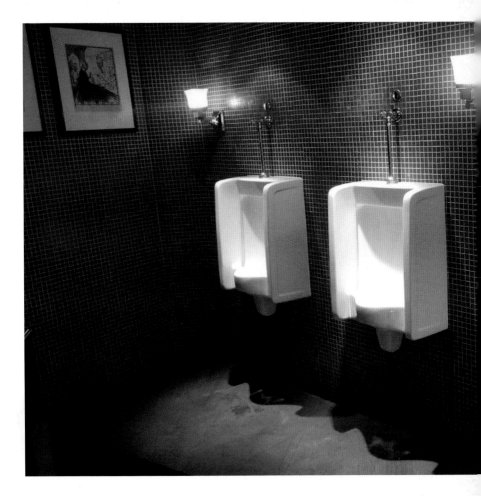

THE IVY

Oh, the hundreds of VIP-ers who
must have shared a swanky siphon
here since the Ivy opened its doors
and U-bends in 1917! Laurence
Olivier and Noël Coward, Tom
Cruise and Brad Pitt, Damien Hirst
and David Beckham – big shots
all, standing shoulder to shoulder
for a superstar slash.

the-ivy.co.uk

THE KNIGHTS TEMPLAR

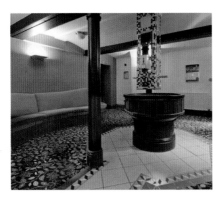

Ladies, meet Myrtle, as she's called, the
nipple-flashing nymph welcoming you to the
loos of The Knights Templar on Chancery
Lane. The pub, named after the bruiser
monks who were once a big noise in these
parts, was originally the Union Bank, so why
not open an account here and make a small
or large deposit.

jdwetherspoon.com

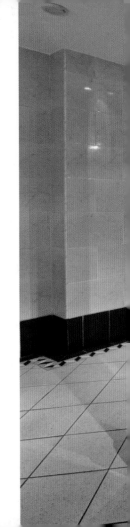

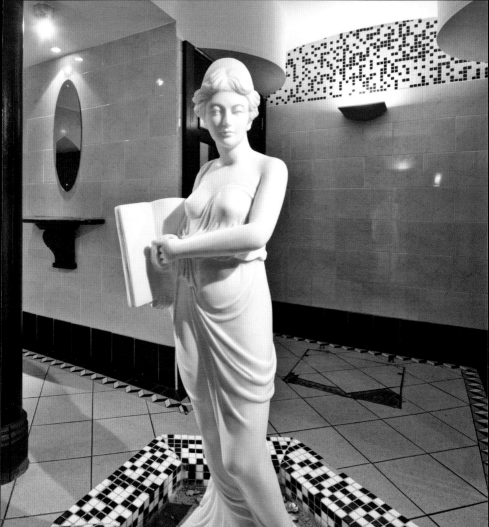

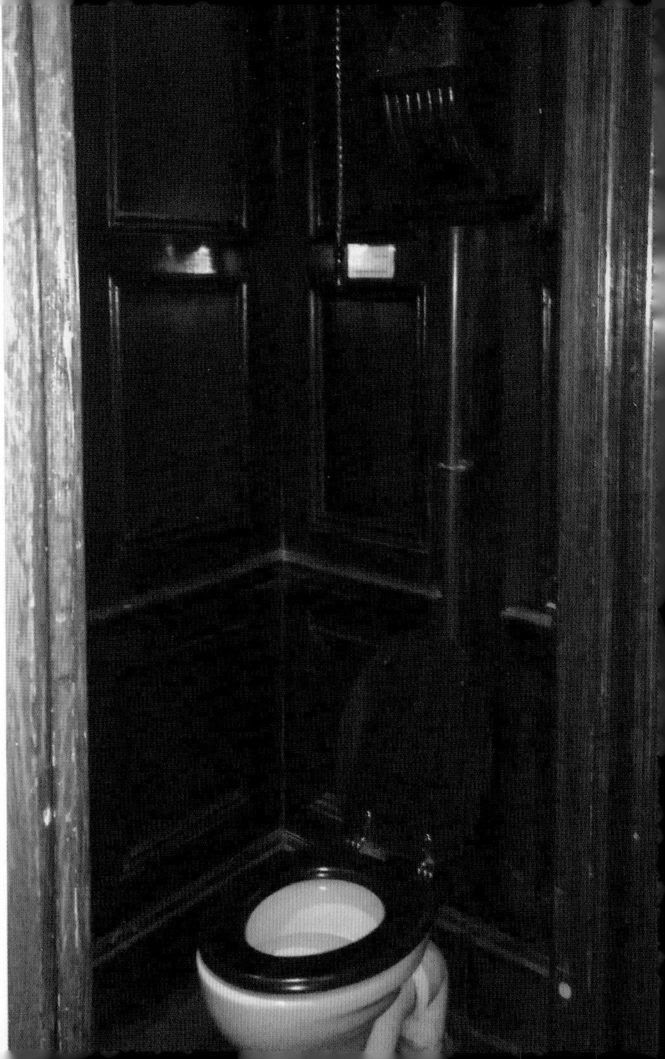

LONDON COLISEUM

A khazi fit for a king – a large one at that,
with a big appetite for fine wine, food and
floozies. So you'd want to get in there before
him – Edward VII, that is, who had this wood-
tastic toilet built for his right royal rump at the
Coliseum theatre, so he could drop a quick
one in the interval and still have time to wet
his whiskers before curtain up.

londoncoliseum.org

MAGGIE'S

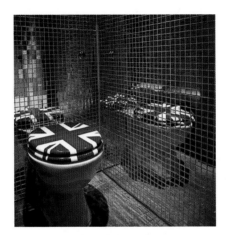

Union Jack? My arse. Where better to have
a patriotic poo than at Maggie's nightclub in
Mayfair, letting go as you listen to piped-in
recordings of Maggie Thatcher letting herself
go – verbally. As the great lady herself said,
'We can do business together.'

maggies-club.com

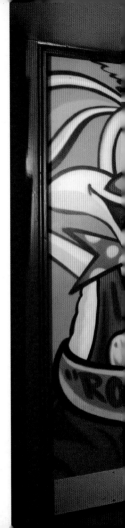

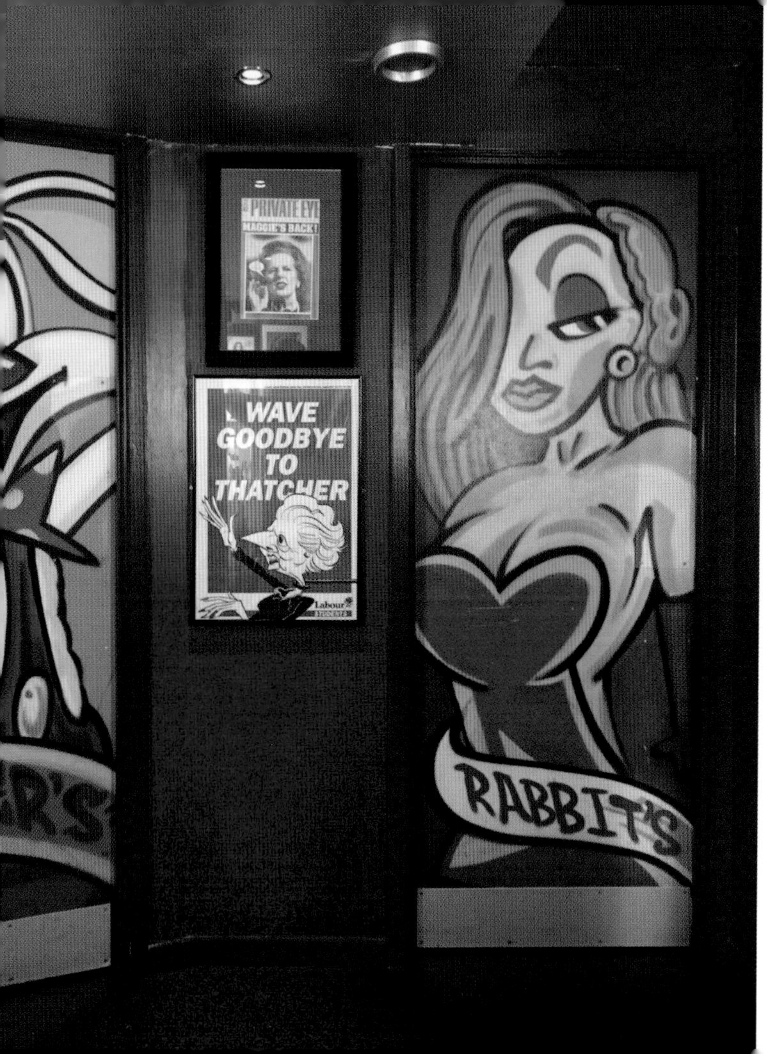
MAGGIE'S BACK!
WAVE
GOODBYE
TO
THATCHER
Labour
RABBIT'S

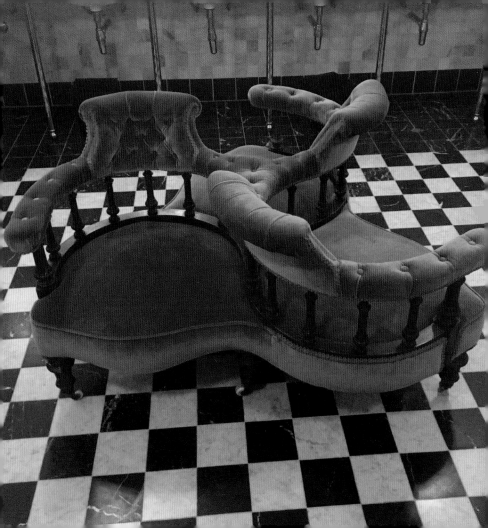

THE NED

Hit the five-star Ned hotel in the heart of
the City, and you can not only lash one
out in the lavvy lap of luxury, but also
recline and enjoy the view from this kinky
Victorian three-way chair. This was once
the headquarters of the Midland Bank,
so somewhere safe to stash your crown
jewels once you've finished with them.

thened.com

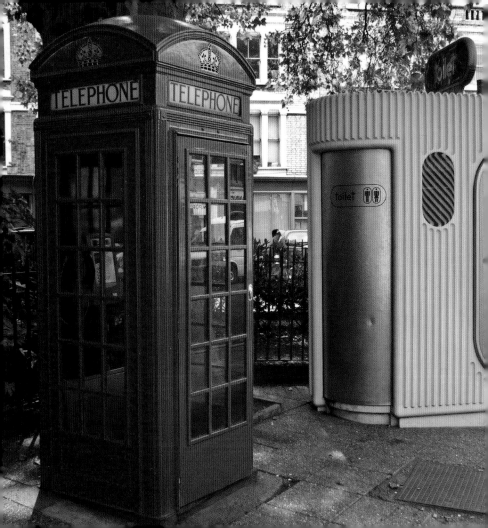

WHEN IN ROMAN LONDON ...

Oi, Nero, put that fiddle down and pass the wet wipe! The Romans may have been clever bastards, but the best they could come up with in the absence of bog roll was a soggy sponge on the end of a stick. In old Londinium town, the Billingsgate Roman Baths, beneath Lower Thames Street, would have seen plenty of bum-buffing.

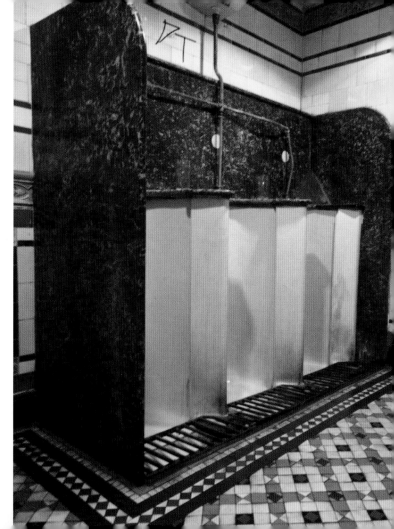

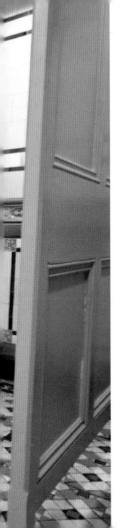

PRINCESS LOUISE

This is the story of the princess and the pee – the Princess Louise pub, in fact, and her marvellous marble urinals. They were the work of architect James Chitty, who employed some of the finest khazi craftsmen of his day. So, if you want to do a shitty in memory of Chitty or point Percy at porcelain perfection, then head Holborn way. Perfect for a night on the tiles.

princesslouisepub.co.uk

SARASTRO

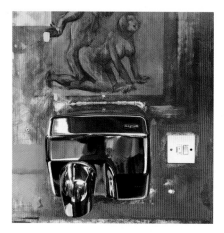

F**king hell! You don't expect to face the Devil dipping his wick as you blow-dry your hands. But then this is Sarastro, a wildly decadent Drury Lane eatery, complete with ten opera boxes, exotic furnishings – and shagtastic loos. But take care, ladies – that horny beast is watching your behind.

sarastro-restaurant.com

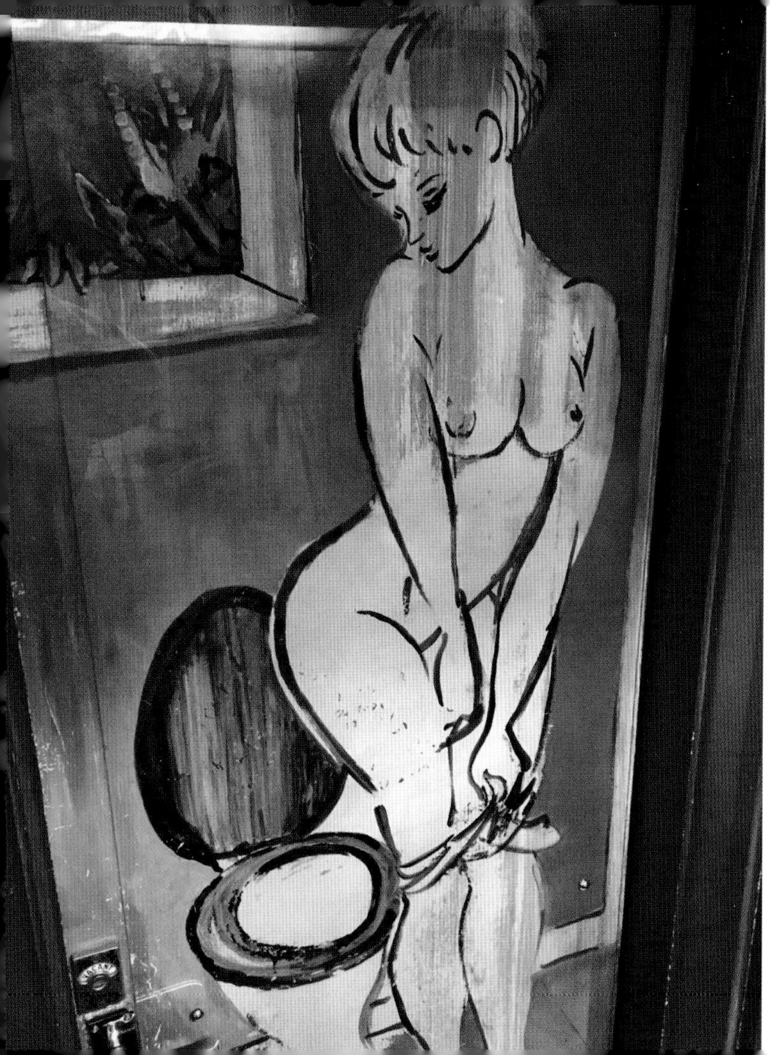

SEXY FISH

Now wash your hands, please.
Well, don't mind if I do, when
the post-pee digits get this
kind of loo-xuriant treatment.
No expense has been spared
on the marble-lous toilet
trappings at Mayfair's Sexy Fish
restaurant. The only crabs you'll
catch here will be the ones on
the menu.

sexyfish.com

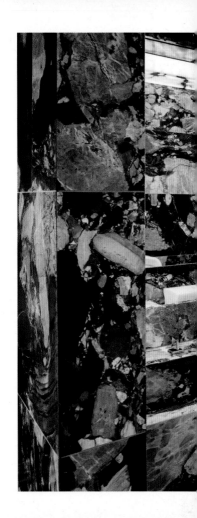

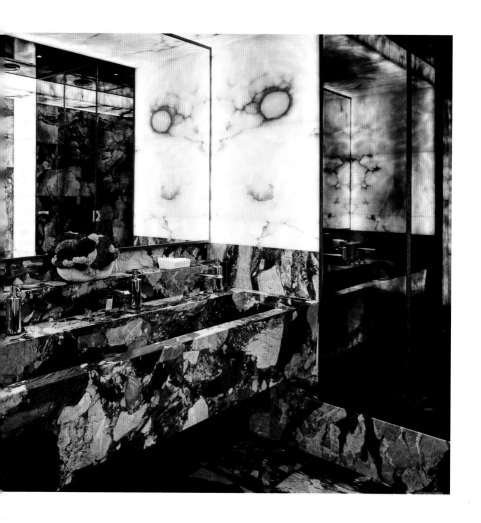

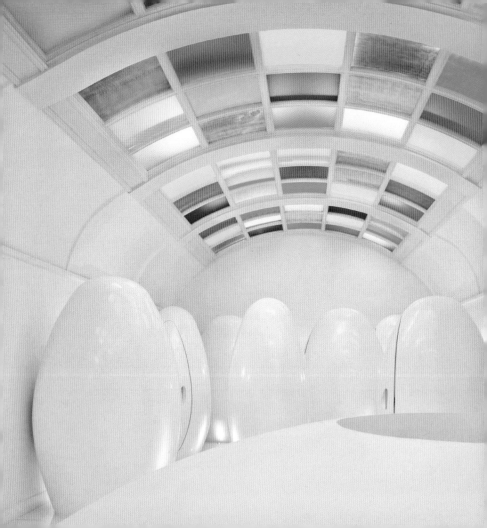

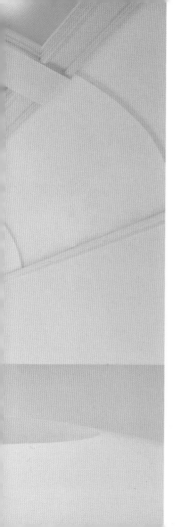

SKETCH

Like pees in a pod? Then
make a wee-line for the Sketch
restaurant loos. There are 16
egg-like crapsules, the work of
French designer and sculptor
Noé Duchaufour-Lawrance,
where both boys and girls – one
at a time, mind – can have a
wacky wazz. Not one for the
khazi-claustrophobic.

sketch.london

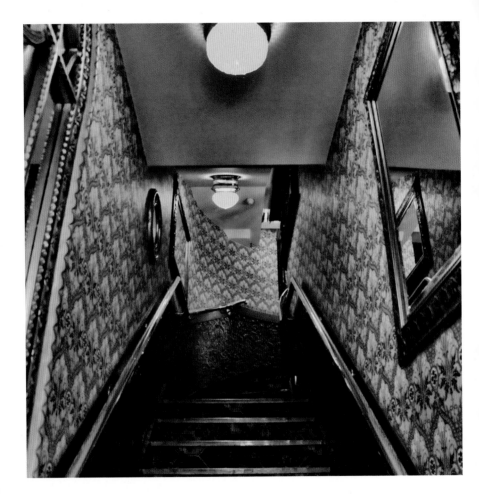

ST STEPHEN'S TAVERN

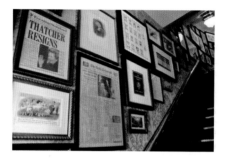

Sometimes it's not the loo but the route to it that gets the waterworks twitching in anticipation. St Stephen's Tavern, the closest pub to the Houses of Parliament, was built in 1873 and has kept most of its Victorian fittings. So let your Big Ben strike and enjoy a prime ministerial pee where the likes of Winston Churchill, Stanley Baldwin and Harold Macmillan have all worked the lower chamber.

ststephenstavern.co.uk

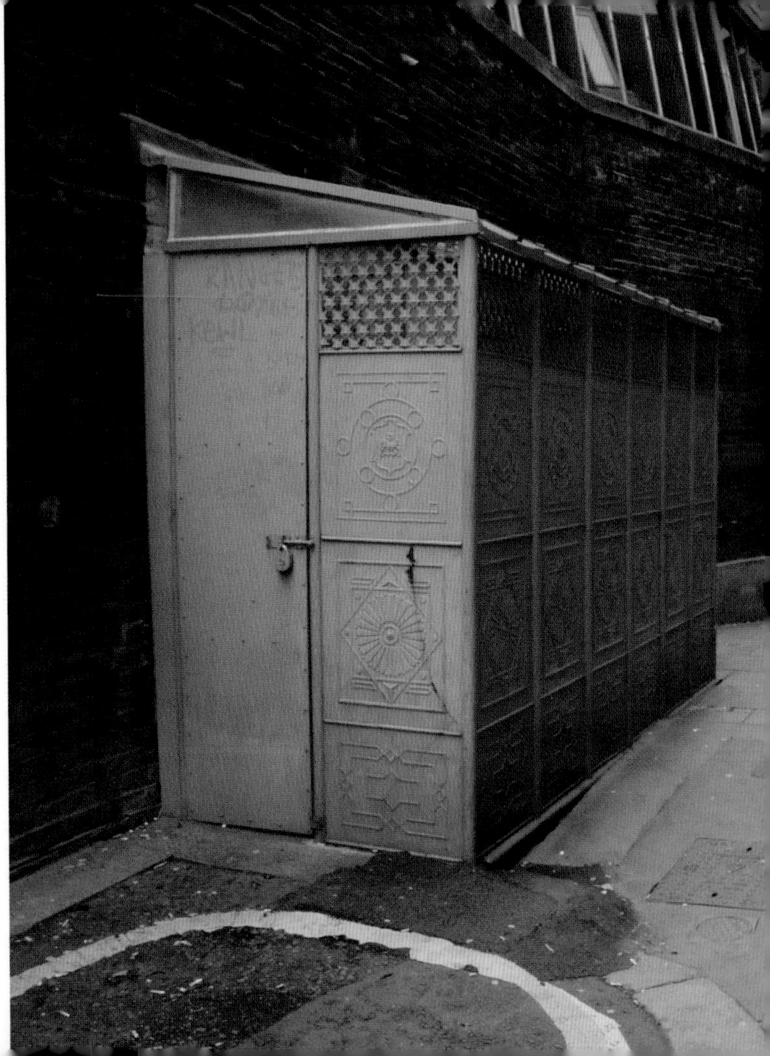

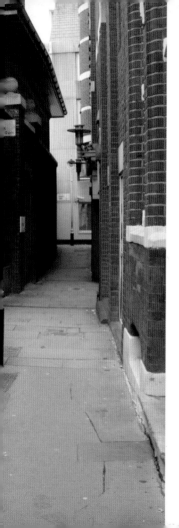

STAR YARD

A handy john for judges or bog
for barristers, the jolly green
Parisian-style pissoir in Star
Yard, off Chancery Lane, is only
a turd's throw from Lincoln's Inn.
Four legal lashers or members of
the jury can hang out at any one
time in the wrought-iron Victorian
khazi, which is still lit by gas
(mains, not men's).

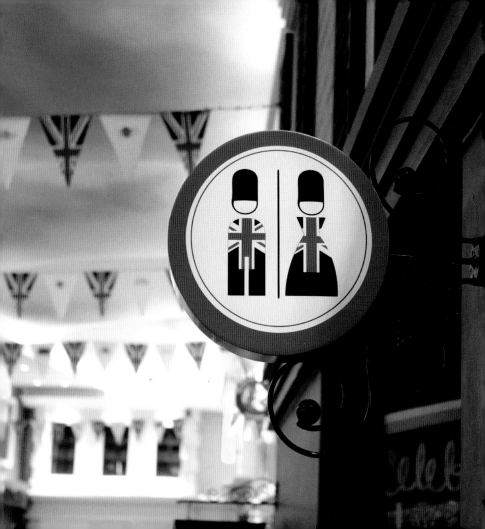

DYING FOR A CRAP

Elvis wasn't the only one to peg out on the pot, you know. In October 1760, 76-year-old King George II popped into the little boys' room at Kensington Palace just after his morning hot chocolate; as the writer Horace Walpole later described it, 'all his actions were invariably methodic'. Sadly this was the King's last, er, movement: hearing a crash, his valet rushed in to find the crowned head dead.

FAR ROCKAWAY

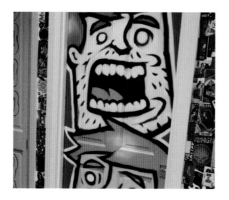

Aaaargh! What's that in the toilet?! Plant a
log in the loo at funky Far Rockaway and
a mighty tree doth grow. It seems to be
dropping big apples, which figures, as this
Shoreditch bar and restaurant is inspired
by New York City street art and culture. So,
wieners at the ready, for a full-on Yankee
doodle dangle.

farrockaway.co.uk

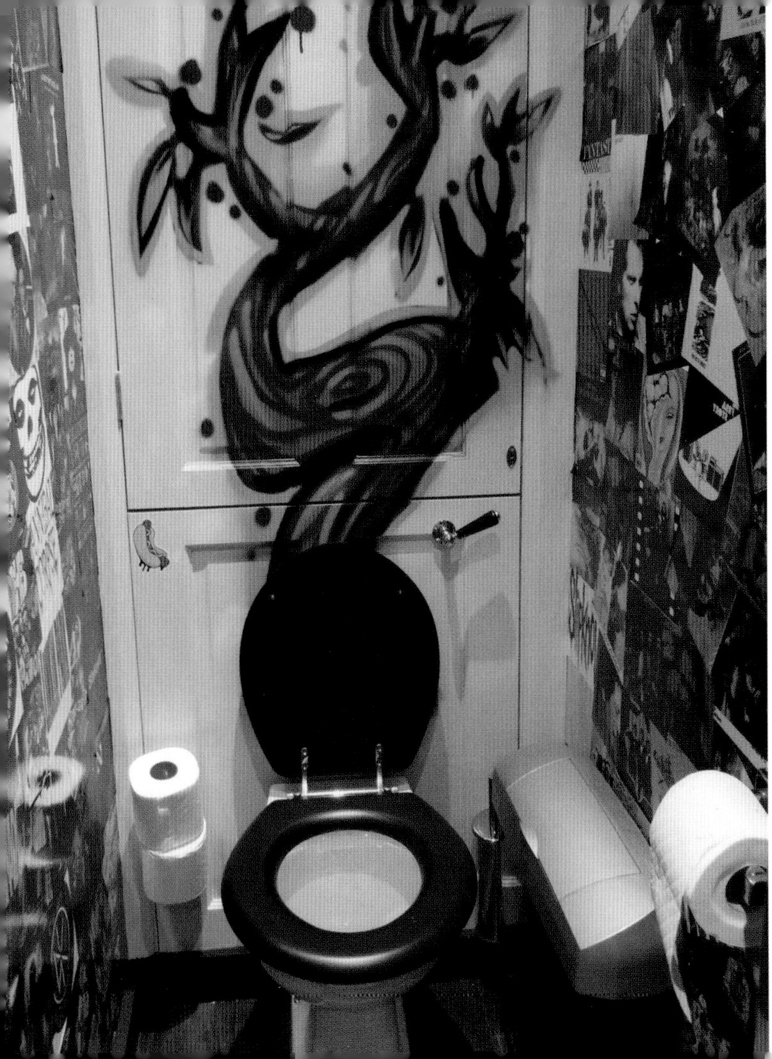

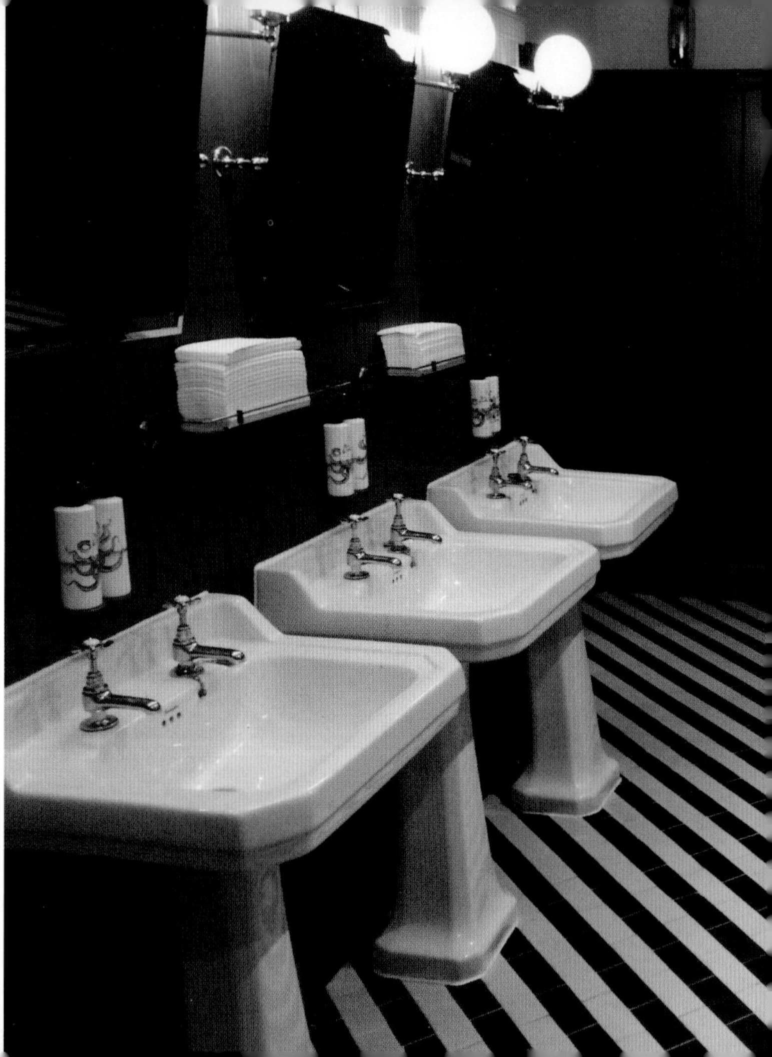

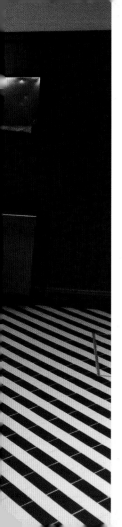

THE HOXTON

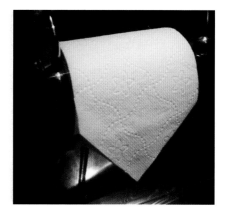

For one of the coolest craps or swankiest slashes in town, it has to be Shoreditch and it has to be the loos at The Hoxton. It's where any caught-short bearded hipster would feel happy to enjoy an on-trend tinkle after a particularly satisfying craft-beer session.

thehoxton.com

THE HUNTER S

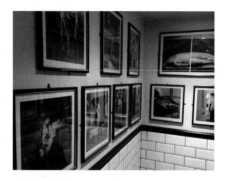

This is peeing as porno. Take care in the gents at The Hunter S pub or you may find more than your spirits raised. Do you look up at the scantily clad lovelies or down into the deep-throat urinals? Or just shut your eyes and count to 100? Hardly surprising that the joint is named after Hunter S. Thompson, the fast, loose and louche author of *Fear and Loathing in Las Vegas*.

thehunter-s.co.uk

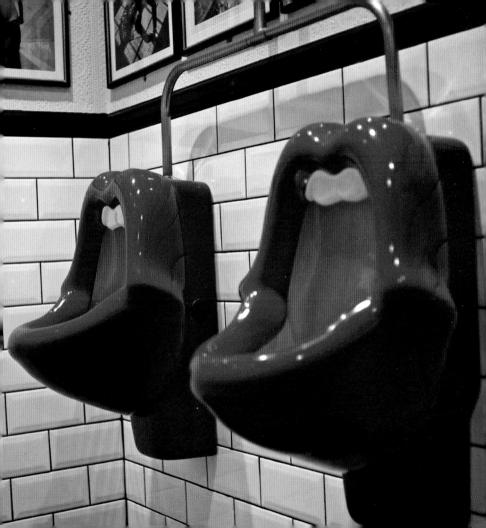

WHERE THERE'S MUCK ...

John Nevil Maskelyne invented the
coin-operated toilet lock in London
in 1892. Only a penny could open
his cunningly devised contraption.
As a professional magician and
escapologist, he must have saved
himself a fortune.

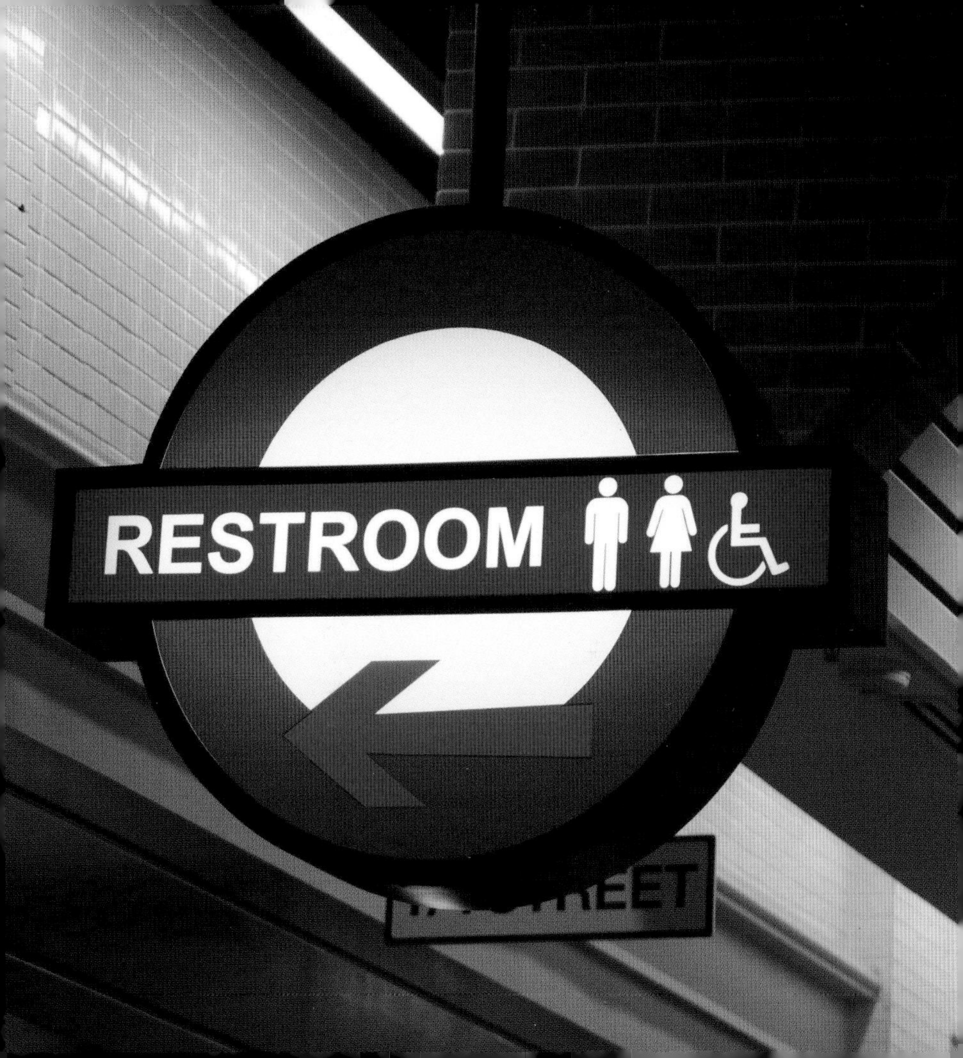
RESTROOM

THE JONES
FAMILY PROJECT

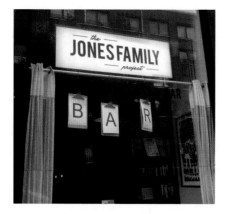

Mirror, mirror on the wall: who's the fairest
wazzer of them all? Yes, it's you, you
gorgeous Shoreditch siphoner, taking
a quick bog break from the juicy steak
awaiting you upstairs. White tiles, white
light, dinky white basins – this is possibly
the purest piss East London has to offer.

jonesfamilyproject.co.uk

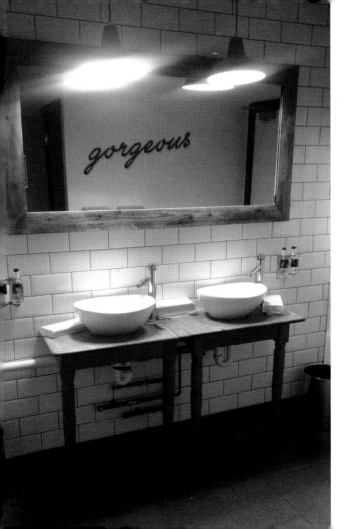

TEN BELLS

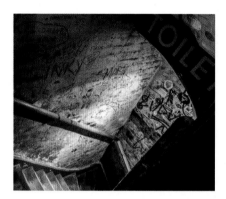

You'd have to be really, really desperate,
right? This is Jack the Ripper territory and
probably what the Devil's own bathroom
looks like. The Ten Bells in Spitalfields, now
spruced up gastropub style, once boasted
London's most graffitied loos. They had a
certain crappy charm, but for these East End
bunker bogs, the writing was on the wall …

tenbells.com

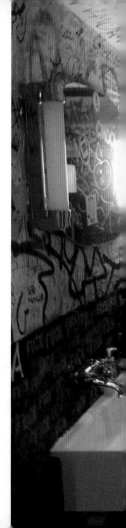

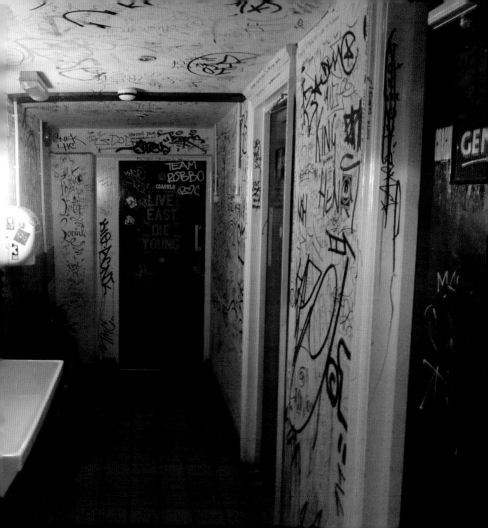

TOWER OF LONDON

The smallest room in the Tower of London's
White Tower is yer genuine Norman khazi
– or garderobe, if you talk like a Norman
– possibly once warmed by the arse of
William the Conqueror himself. It's basically
a hole in the floor, so careful as you walk
underneath, unless you want to encounter
a Richard III.

hrp.org.uk/tower-of-london

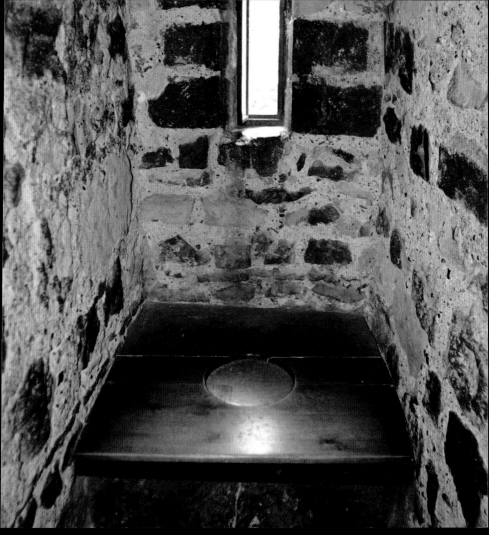

WESLEY'S CHAPEL

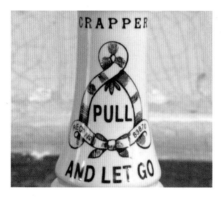

You won't have a more pleasing pee. These gents put the John into John Wesley, the founder of Methodism, whose City Road chapel squats over a row of red and black marble urinals, unchanged since 1899. After cleansing your soul above, empty your holy spirit below on a genuine Thomas Crapper crapper. It's number-two heaven.

wesleyschapel.org.uk

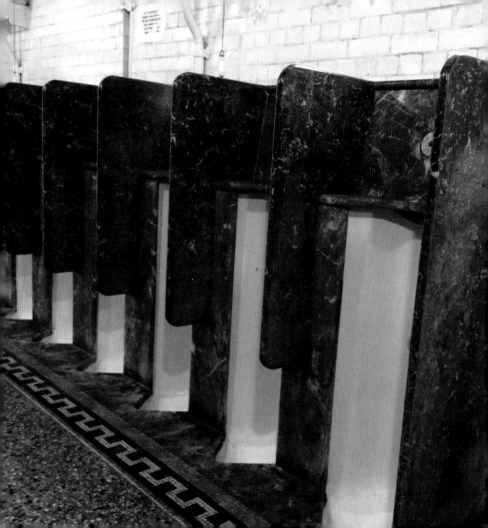

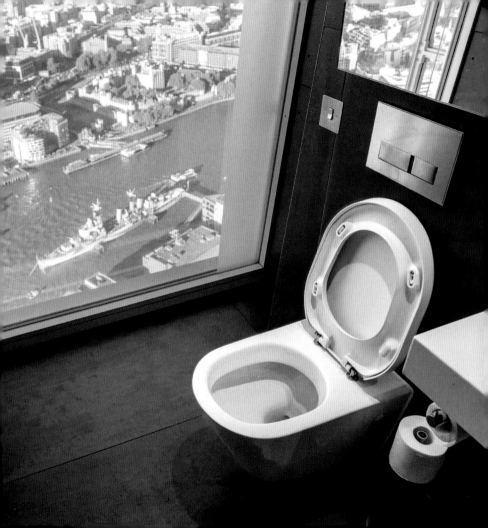

IN FOR A PENNY ...

Victorians went ape for 'monkey closets', the world's first public toilets, when they debuted in 1851 at the Great Exhibition in Hyde Park. The loos were the brainchild of Brighton plumber George Jennings, who charged visitors one penny in return for a clean seat, a towel and a comb, and even threw in a shoe-shine for the gents. The euphemism 'to spend a penny' soon caught on. Wonder what you got for sixpence?

CERU

If you've never let one go in the Levant
(that's the Eastern Med for those slackers
who didn't get their geography GCSE),
then hitch up the camel train for South
Kensington's CERU restaurant. Once you've
left your own little piece of Eastern promise
beyond the exotic doors and charmed the
snake back into the basket, you'll probably
find the tiles quite Moorish.

cerurestaurants.com

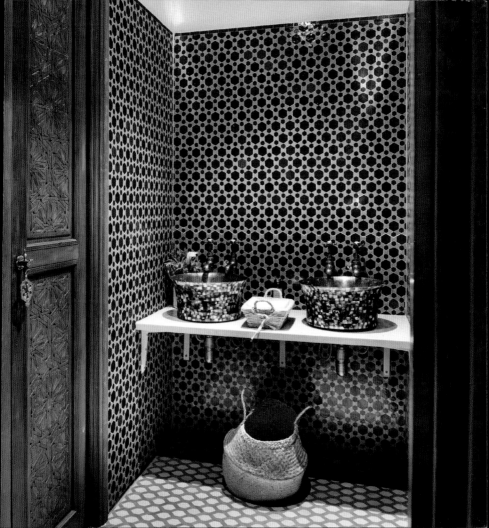

GINGLIK

Once upon a time, laughs in a loo were
rare, beyond sniggering at the bloke next
to you or hiding all the toilet paper. Then
along came the Ginglik club, squeezed into
a sunken Edwardian public convenience
built to serve caught-short spectators of the
1908 Olympics at nearby White City, and
suddenly you could piss yourself good and
proper at one of their comedy nights. Sadly
it's now closed – flushed down the pan of
hilarity history.

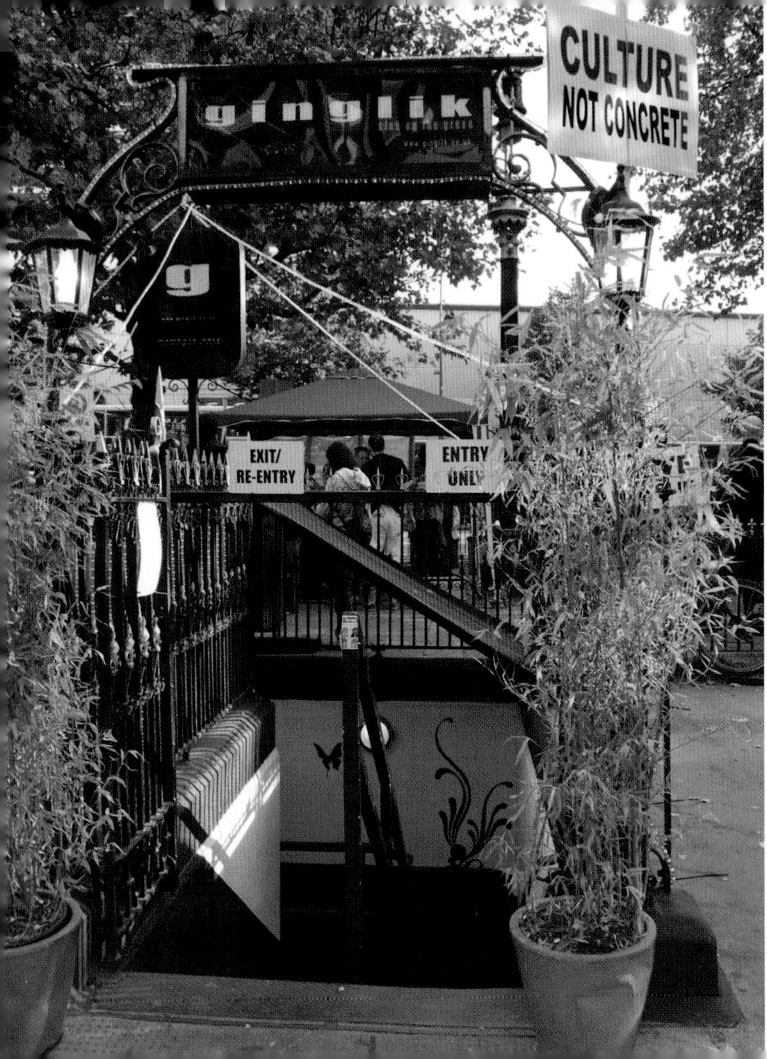
CULTURE
NOT CONCRETE
ginglik
g
EXIT/
RE-ENTRY
ENTRY
ONLY

HARRODS

Once you've offloaded a
ton of cash in Harrods of
Knightsbridge, it's time to
splash out or drop a packet
in the mahogany-and-marble
plushness of the men's loos.
The department store, built in
1905, has 13 loos over its 4.5
acres, so go ahead: shop until
you need to drop.

harrods.com

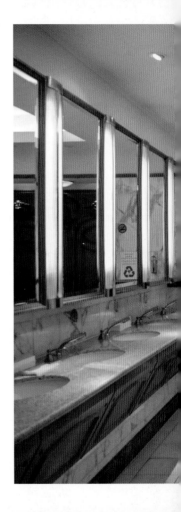

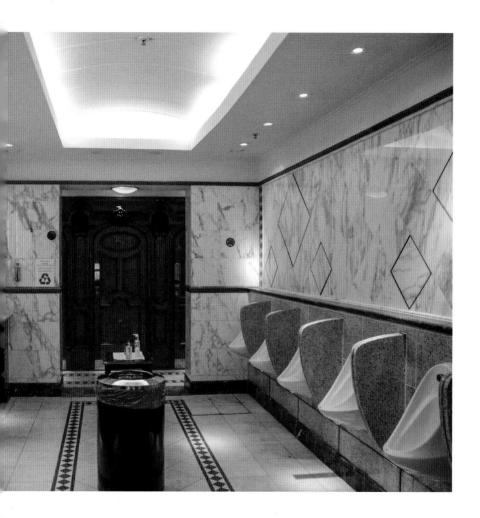

MARYLEBONE STATION

There's no monopoly in London on Monopoly-themed loos (see The Castle, page 12). The difference here, though, is that you're actually piddling in a real Monopoly property, Marylebone Station. If you aim high enough, you can stake your claim on Marylebone Station itself – or, more realistically, just piss on your Chances.

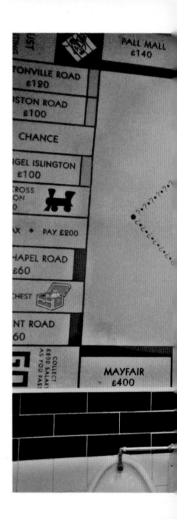

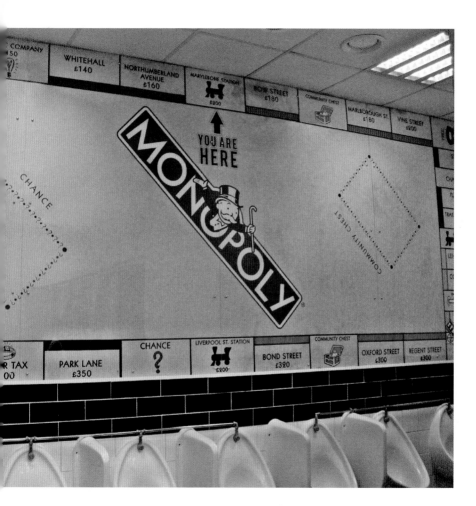

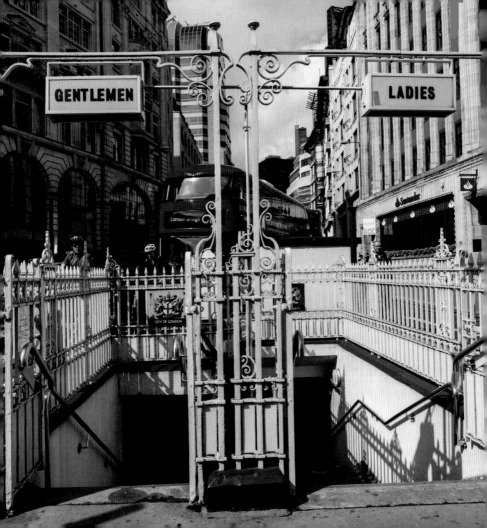

OUR GREAT CRAPITAL

If you think that smells bad … In
July and August 1858, London
was up to its arse in what became
known as the Great Stink. At the
time, the city used the Thames as
one great shitter, and in the summer
heat the raw sewage and industrial
filth turned into the world's worst
bog smog. Curtains at the riverside
Houses of Parliament had to be
soaked in lime chloride to hide the
pong, and MPs even thought about
running the country from ordure-
free Oxford.

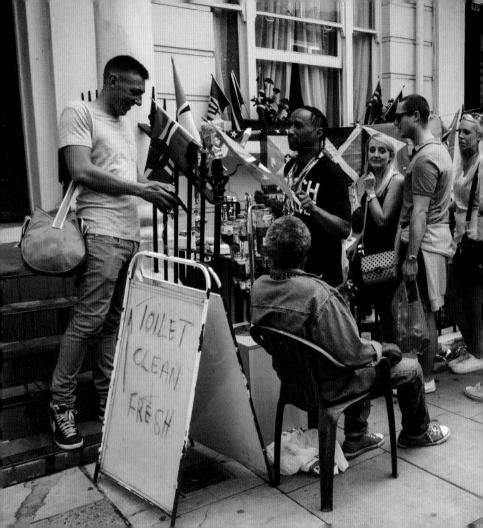

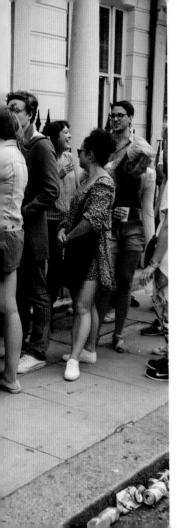

NOTTING HILL CARNIVAL

If you go down to the Notting
Hill Carnival today ... you'd
better tie a knot in it. This is
toilet hell. Blokes, of course,
can – and will – wazz their way
through the streets of West
London. Girls – well, join the
Portaloo queue and wait until
your bladder explodes.

thelondonnottinghillcarnival.com

VICTORIA & ALBERT MUSEUM

Ever wondered where Queen Victoria
fulfilled her royal doodies? Then piddle
down to the Victoria & Albert Museum in
Kensington to sit, nay shit, where our very
own Empress of India rested her orb and
sceptre. The luxurious lav was specially
built for Vicky in case she ever felt dicky
on a royal visit.

vam.ac.uk

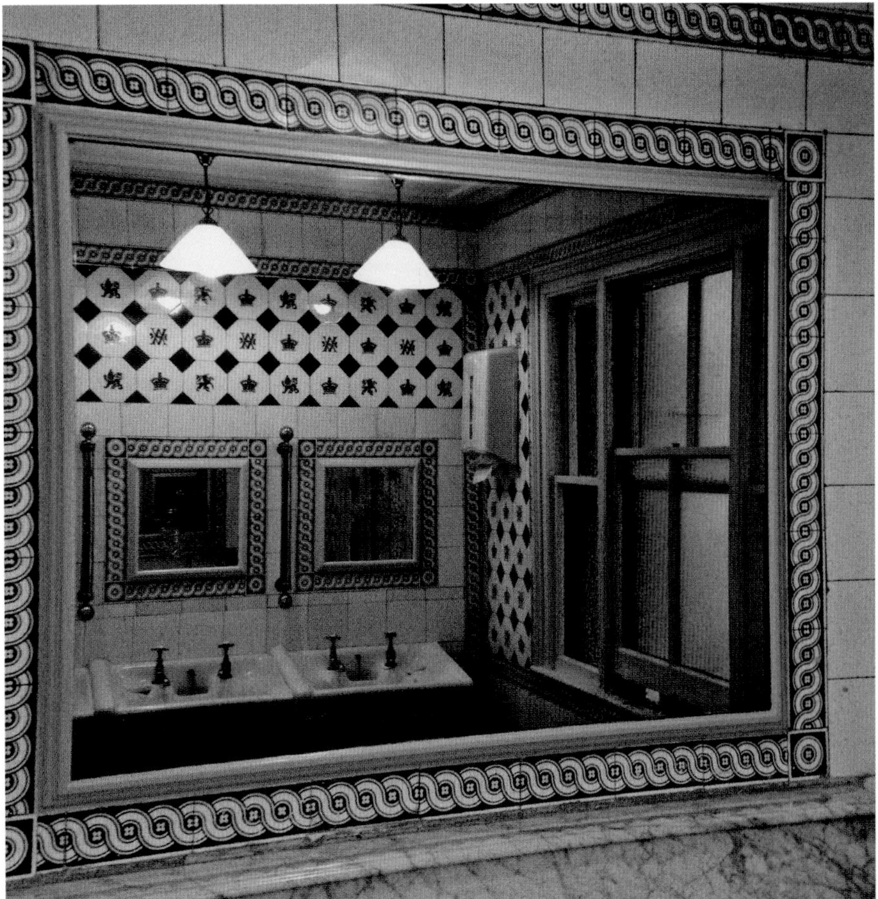

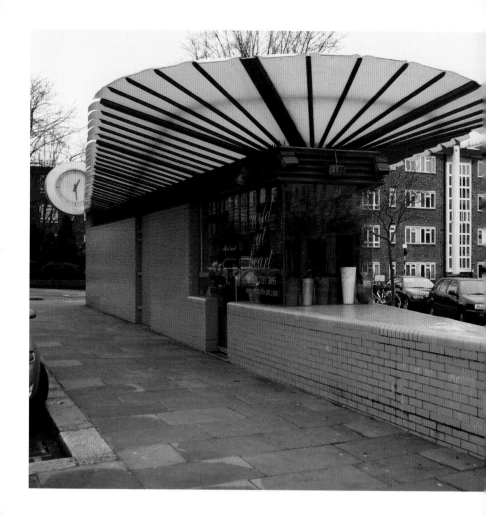

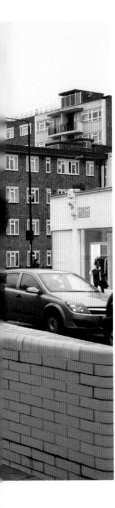

WESTBOURNE GROVE

This has got to be the sweetest-smelling loo in London. At the sharp end of the Westbourne Grove lavs in Notting Hill, opened in 1993, is a florist's, while the wider end hosts a different kind of business altogether. The council's original design was such crap that the locals commissioned their own convenience – a turquoise triangle, flushed with fragrance.

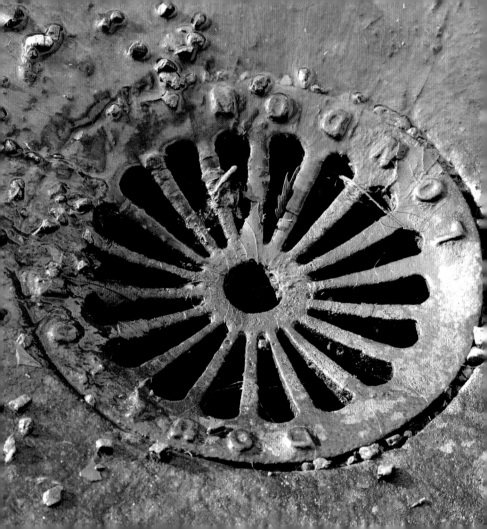

THIS CITY'S FULL OF TOSHERS

In Victorian London, enterprising little urchins could make a decent wedge as 'toshers', or sewer scavengers. Risking their lives to slosh around all night in other people's crap, toshers looked for coins and other precious lost property, but grabbed anything that could be cleaned and sold. This work was illegal and secretive, but toshers stood out from the crowd thanks to the long hooked poles they carried around to save themselves when they got into really deep shit.

Thank you to everyone who took or supplied photos, particularly the loo-owners themselves. Any omissions below will gratefully be rectified.

---

10 9 8 7 6 5 4 3 2 1

Pop Press, an imprint of
Ebury Publishing,
20 Vauxhall Bridge Road,
London SW1V 2SA

Pop Press is part of the Penguin Random
House group of companies whose
addresses can be found at global.
penguinrandomhouse.com

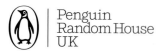
Penguin
Random House
UK

Text by John Andrews © Pop Press 2018
Photographs © individual photographers
Design by Ben Gardiner
Project management by whitefox

First published by Pop Press in 2018

www.penguin.co.uk

A CIP catalogue record for this book
is available from the British Library

ISBN 9781785037511

Colour origination by BORN
Printed and bound in China
by Toppan Leefung

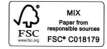

Penguin Random House is committed
to a sustainable future for our business,
our readers and our planet. This book is
made from Forest Stewardship Council®
certified paper